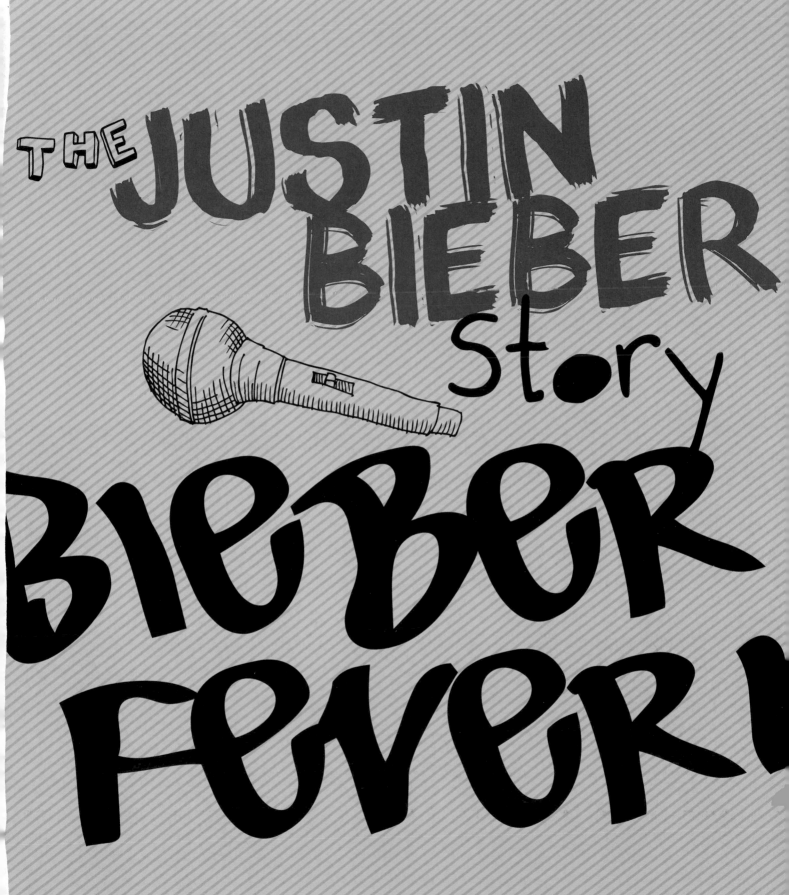

THE JUSTIN BIEBER Story

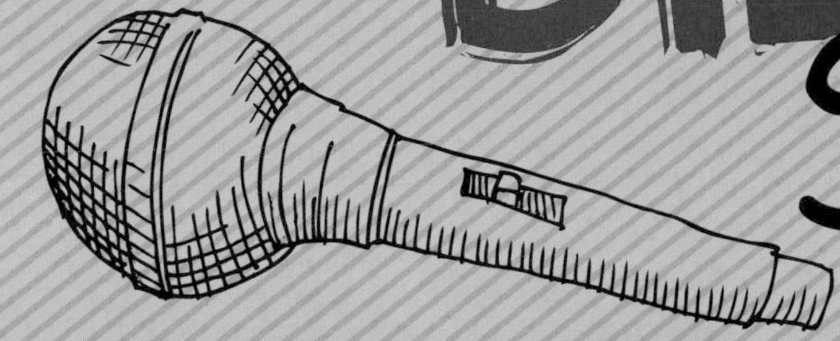

BIEBER FEVER!

Parragon
Bath · New York · Singapore · Hong Kong · Cologne · Delhi · Melbourne

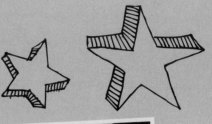

Author; Lisa Clark
Published by Parragon in 2010
Parragon
Queen Street House
4 Queen Street
Bath
BA1 1HE
UK

ISBN: 978-1-4454-0685-5

Printed in China

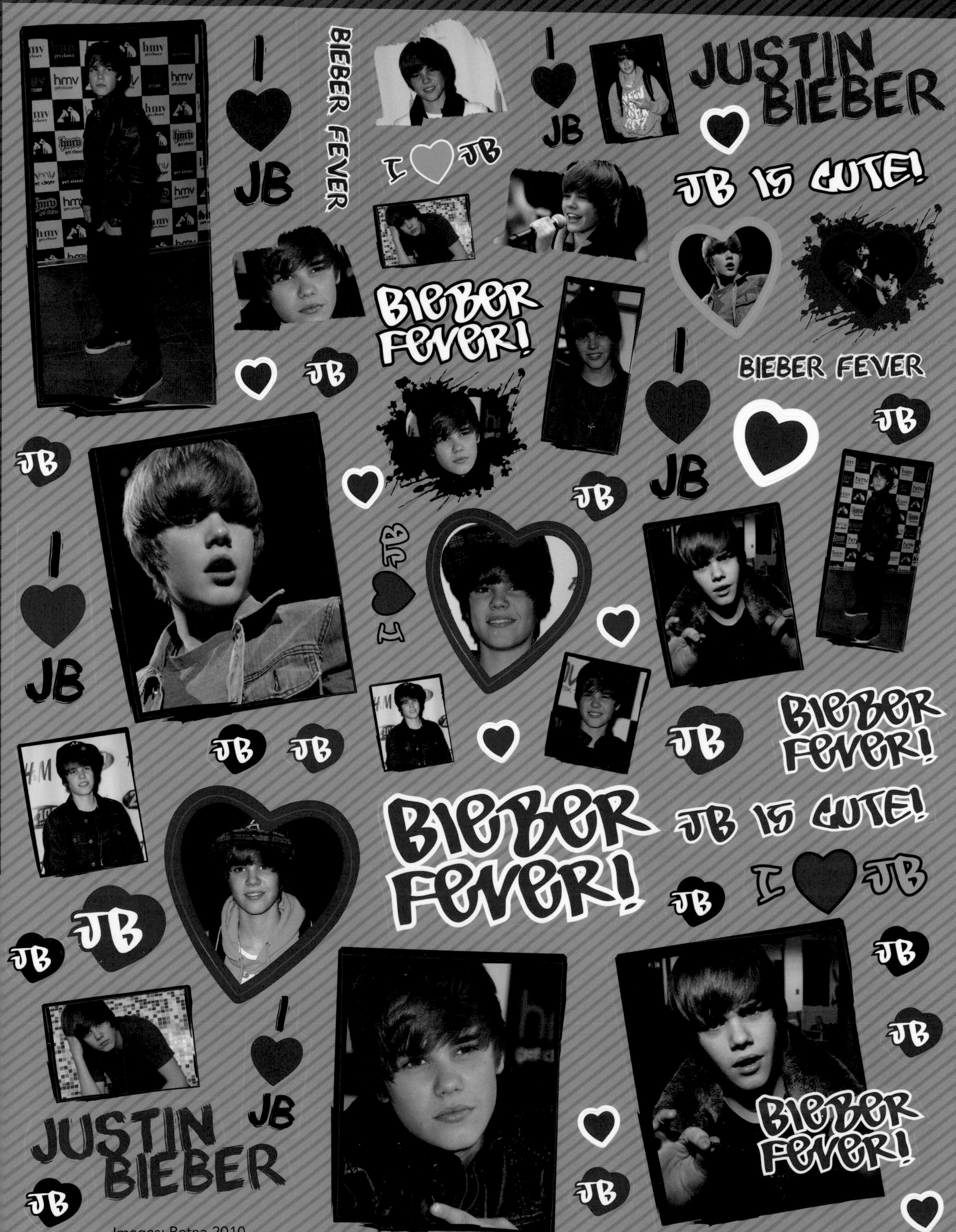

Images: Retna 2010

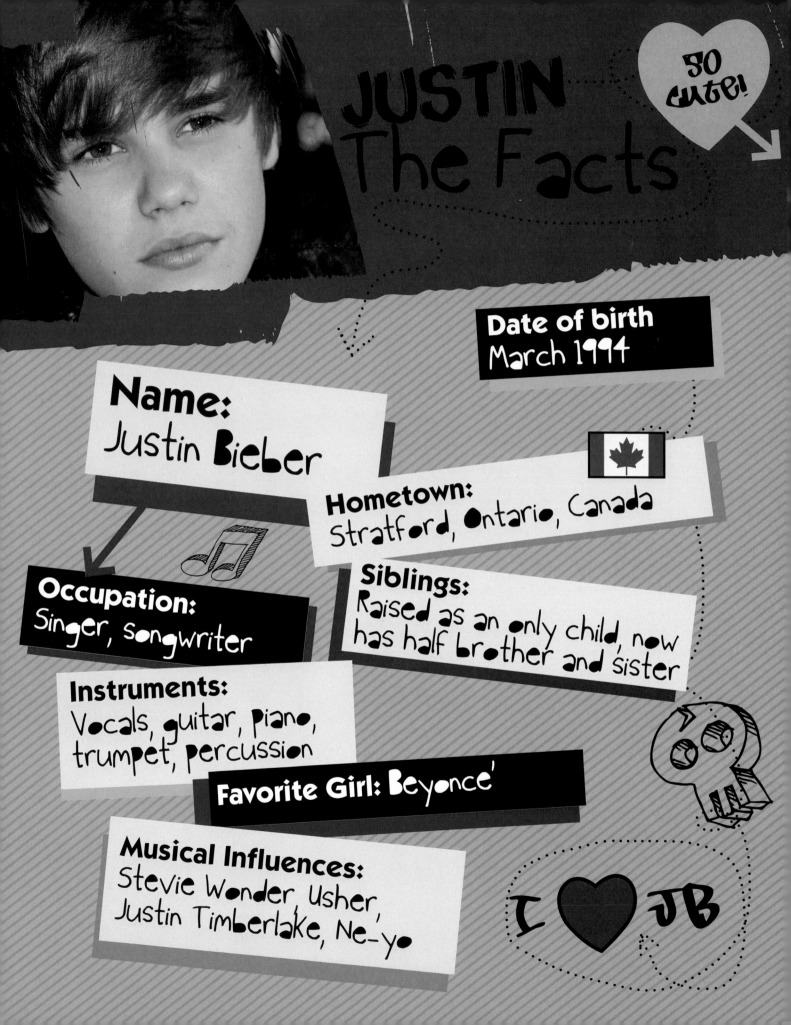

JUSTIN The Facts

SO CUTE!

Date of birth
March 1994

Name:
Justin Bieber

Hometown:
Stratford, Ontario, Canada

Occupation:
Singer, songwriter

Siblings:
Raised as an only child, now has half brother and sister

Instruments:
Vocals, guitar, piano, trumpet, percussion

Favorite Girl: Beyoncé

Musical Influences:
Stevie Wonder, Usher, Justin Timberlake, Ne-yo

I ♥ JB

It only takes one listen to this cute 16 year-old to realize that he is a soul-singing phenomenon—want to know how Justin hit the big time? READ ON...

TOP

"I started singing about three years ago," says the Canadian native who grew up an only child in Stratford, Ontario. "I entered a local singing competition called Stratford Idol. The other people in the competition had been taking singing lessons and had vocal coaches. I wasn't taking it too seriously at the time, I would just sing around the house. I was only 12 and I got second place."

To share his success with his family and friends, Justin began posting his performance footage online in 2007. "I put my singing videos from the competition on YouTube so that my friends and family could watch them," he says. "But it turned out that other people liked them and they started subscribing to them. That's how my manager found me. He saw me on YouTube and contacted my family and now I'm signed!"

TALENT

- Bieber put his impeccable spin on songs from artists like Usher, Ne-Yo and Stevie Wonder.
- Justin racked up over 100,000,000 views on YouTube purely from word of mouth.
- Both Justin Timberlake and Usher wanted to sign Justin to their record labels, but in 2008, Justin officially signed to Island Records, a dream come true for the teen, making Usher his musical mentor.
- His debut album, My World has been produced by The Dream and Tricky Stewart who produced "Umbrella" for Rihanna and Beyoncé's Single Ladies (Put A Ring On It).

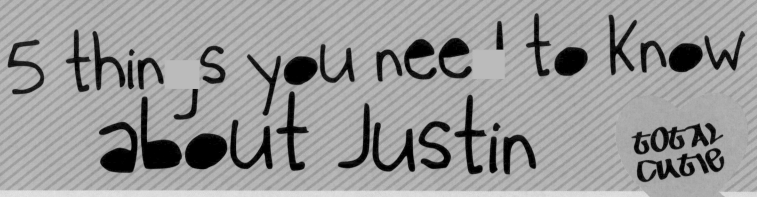

5 things you need to Know about Justin

total cutie

Here are five things you didn't know about the YouTube sensation who's making the girls scream over his sweet smile and even sweeter voice...

1. He was raised in Canada, but currently lives in Atlanta, America

"I grew up in Stratford, Ontario," he says. "It's a little town of like 30,000 people." He's since moved to Atlanta with his mother to record and learn from his mentor Usher, who also resides in Atlanta. "Usher is like a big brother," says Bieber.

2. He's single!

"I'm single and ready to mingle," he proclaims. When he was asked if he was shocked by the amount of attention he's been receiving from ladies, Justin replied, "Not really. It's awesome. What 15-year-old boy wouldn't want girls chasing after them all day long?"

3. He's pals with Taylor Swift

"We talk on AIM and I text her every once in a while," Bieber says about the country singer. "We're friends. Taylor is a really nice person."

4. He wants to go to college

"I have a tutor," he says. "I want to go to college, I think it would be a blast."

5. He plays four instruments

He's a whiz on the guitar, piano, drums and trumpet. And though he's pretty sure picking up another instrument would be difficult, he says he's up for the challenge, "It would be cool to learn the violin."

MY WORLD

What it's like to live in the world of Justin 24/7...

Justin hasn't always lived like a celeb...

"...I wasn't poor, but I definitely didn't have a lot of money. I couldn't afford to get a lot of new clothes a lot of times. But I had a roof over my head. I was very fortunate. I had my grandparents, I saw them a lot, they were very kind. So I grew up getting everything that I wanted."

Justin is close with his buds...

"...My friends are very supportive. I have two really close friends—Ryan and Chaz. They're really close to me, but they really don't care about any of this. They like me for me. When we're hanging out and I say something stupid or something, they're not going to treat me like I'm a superstar, by any means. They're not going to treat me like I'm bigger than everybody else. They're just going to treat me like Justin. They're going to pop me in the head and not care. I get to see them at least once a month. I get to fly them out to wherever I am. I've flown them out to L.A. and Atlanta. I think it's really important to just have your close friends around you. We're very active, we play basketball and hockey and soccer and stuff. We go to the movies with girls and stuff like regular teenage boys."

Justin has a 'swagger' coach...

"...he helps me to just stay swaggerific. It's confidence, it's style, I don't know how else to put it. It's swagger. It's a word."

STYLIN' The Justin way

Skinny jeans, hoodie, backpack and cap—too cool for school.

A cute scarf, simple white tee and a New York skyline...

The ultimate Justin accessory is a skateboard!

Justin rocks the pop star staples—sunglasses and a guitar!

Girls, girls, girls

You've only got to listen to Justin's lyrics to know that he loves the ladies—but who does he crush on? What does he think of his fans and what does he look for in a girlfriend?

Justin hearts Beyoncé...

"I got to meet her at the VMAs. She was very nice, very beautiful and very bootylicious. She's even hotter in person actually. Jay Z was there but I got to flirt with her a little bit anyway. I don't remember exactly what I said in the heat of the moment, but I remember she definitely flirted back!"

His first kiss...

"I was 13 when I had my first kiss. We dated for a little bit."

Justin's ideal girl...

"...I look for a girl with nice eyes and a big smile, and a girl who's funny because I like to laugh a lot!.." He loves being followed by girls.. "Seriously, who wouldn't?! I love it! It's amazing. I didn't really expect any of it so it's been a blast..."

Bieber Fever

The pop sensation on fame, touring and the highs and lows of being a popstar...

Justin broke his foot on stage in the UK but still finished the song—hero!

"...It was a lot of fun. I mean my foot broke at the beginning of the song—I was running and there was a little dip in the stage and I rolled my ankle real bad and broke it—so it was definitely a struggle to finish the song. But I really didn't want to let my fans down and they were looking for a show so I had to give it to them..."

He loves being the centre of attention...

"...I'm definitely in the right business, I've always loved to be the centre of attention. In class I would always be the class clown..."

Justin loves YouTube and Twitter

"...I think that the Internet is something that keeps your fans involved in the project. They can talk to you, they can write to you, you're able to interact with your fans, you can keep them updated, you can put videos on YouTube saying where you are, and it just makes them feel like they're part of the project. It's a new day and age. I think a lot of older artists didn't have the chance to use the Internet and Facebook. It's a great way to bring your fans in..."

He wants to duet with Beyoncé...

"...she's just so hot. My favorite Beyoncé song is probably 'Irreplaceable', but my favorite Beyoncé video is definitely 'Single Ladies'"

TODA

THE TUNES

Releases

- One Time
- One Less Lonely Girl
- Love Me
- Favorite girl
- Album: My World
- Baby feat. Ludacris

His first album, *My world* ,has been a huge success. His first single, "One Time" produced by Tricky, is about one of Justin's favorite topics, puppy love.

"...'*One Time*' is basically about being in a typical teen relationship so it's a song everyone can relate to. You know when you're younger and you thought it was love, but then later on you realize it was just puppy love? That's what the song's about...."

Usher joins Justin on "First Dance" where the two share verses on a song that Bieber describes as, "A slow groovy song that people can dance to." On the Midi-Mafia produced "Down to Earth" Justin digs deep to talk about growing up. "Bigger" finds the teenaged singer maturing at a steady rate, while motivating his listeners to strive for their goals.

Twitter with Justin

Justin is an avid Twitter-er - check him out @Justinbieber —here are some of our favorites...

update

What's happening?

@Justinbieber **every1 this weekend let's try and get BABY to #1 on ITUNES!! would b my first #1 and a dream come true. sorry @ taylorswift13 i gotta try ;)**

@Justinbieber **very upset that some of my vids and some of my fans vids are being taken down by youtube. working to fix this now. no 1 messes with my fans!**

@Justinbieber **About to go perform in front of the palace...hope the queen doesn't call in a noise complaint..**

@Justinbieber **little bit of snow in London and they shut the city down. In Canada this wouldn't even get us a school delay**

@Justinbieber **I'm online and see all this support and its amazing. All of u are changing my life everyday and Im extremely grateful. I wanted 2 say thank u**

The Bieber Q&A

How much do you really know about the Canadian-born sweetheart... test your Justin knowledge!

Answers at the bottom of each page!

What was the name of Justin's first single?

When was Justin's album, My World released in the UK?

Is Justin the only artist in Billboard history to have four singles from a debut album hit in the Top 40 of the "Hot 100" before the album was even released?

Where is Justin from?

One Time
January 2010
Yes
Ontario, Canada

The questions you NEED the answers to...Justin spills on Ugg boots, his favorite movies and his guilty pleasures...

When's Justin's birthday?

How many instruments does Justin play?

When you were a kid and you were learning how to sing, who was it that you were trying to emulate?

If you weren't a popstar what job would you do?

Who in your family are you closest to?

What's Justin's favorite sport?

March
Four
I looked up to Michael Jackson and Stevie Wonder and Boyz II Men. But I never tried to sound like anybody
I'd like to be an architect. That would be cool. I like drawing
My mom
Hockey, he supports the Toronto Maple Leafs

I ♥ JB

ISLAND
RAYMOND BRAUN MEDIA GROUP
Hard Rock CAFE
fye
SCHOOL BOY
UNIVERSAL STUDIOS City WALK HOLLYWOOD
AMP RADIO 97.1 FM ALL THE HITS
TIGER beat
BOP
teen island

Who's your celebrity crush?

What girl trend confuses you?

What's the movie that you secretly love?

The Bieber Q&A

Beyoncé. She's awesome

I need to do a song with her — I need to do everything with her

Uggs. I think they're ugly. And I think big sunglasses are kind of overrated. I like big sunglasses but not those huge, round ones

I like The Notebook

The Bieber Q&A

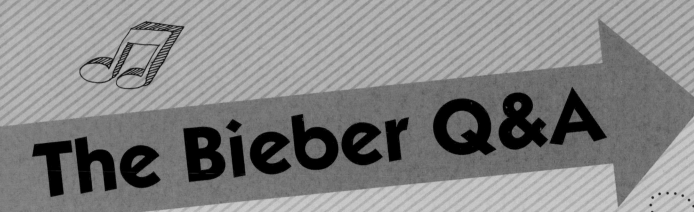

What's your worst habit?

Fill in the blank: When I'm 17 I want to...

What's your TV favorite?

What's the last thing that you bought?

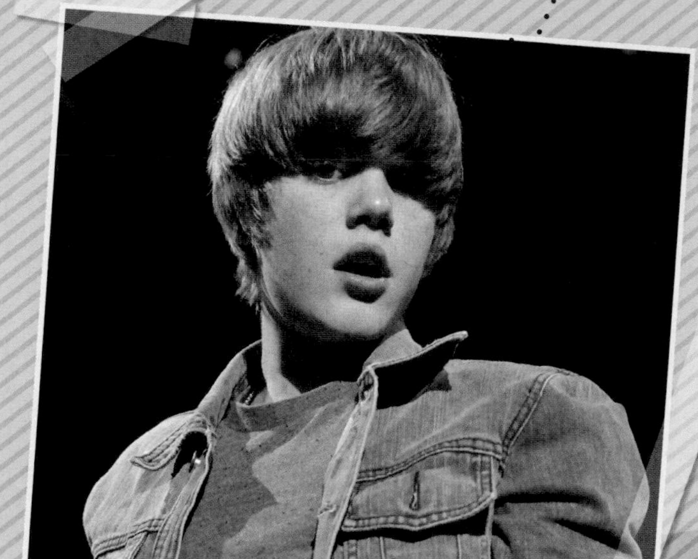

Eating too much candy

... have a second album out and be touring, and hopefully have my own charity by then

I like Smallville. I don't get the chance to watch a lot of TV because I'm busy a lot

The MacBook Pro. It's awesome!

the end